Original title:
Lace and the Light

Copyright © 2025 Creative Arts Management OÜ
All rights reserved.

Author: Gideon Barrett
ISBN HARDBACK: 978-1-80586-185-0
ISBN PAPERBACK: 978-1-80586-657-2

Delicate Networks of Dawn

Threads of giggles weave through air,
Morning antics beyond compare.
Dewdrops glisten, slip and slide,
Chasing sunlight, frolicsome ride.

Breezy whispers tickle the trees,
Squirrels join in, if you please.
Spinning tales with playful grace,
Sunrise chuckles light up the place.

Veils of Morning Glow

Joyful whispers dance and play,
Sunbeams peek in a cheeky way.
Bubbles bounce, their laughter bright,
Chasing shadows out of sight.

A cat in shades, oh what a sight!
Pouncing joyfully, pure delight.
Birds crack jokes in melodies,
Sprinkling humor with morning breeze.

Tapestry of Sunlit Shadows

Patchwork smiles of sunlit beams,
Chasing dreams with wily schemes.
Puppies prance in radiant beams,
Dashing here, oh how it seems!

Tickled grass in bright array,
Wands of light come out to play.
Witty whispers swirl around,
In this silly sunlight found.

Where Shadows Dance with Light

Skirts of shadows swish and sway,
Charmed by sunshine's bright ballet.
Laughing leaves spin in delight,
Whirling time in silly flight.

With each step, a shadow pranks,
Tripping sunlight, laughing flanks.
Together they sway, a prancing crew,
In this world where joy breaks through.

Whimsical Designs Beneath the Stars

Under the night, giggles gleam,
Threads of dreams weave through the seam.
Twirling in shadows, they slip and slide,
A cosmic dance where the quirks reside.

Jumpy patterns in a swirling spree,
Ticklish stars join in, oh so free!
With a wink and a spin, they twirl around,
Creating a tapestry, joyful and sound.

The Constellation of Silken Memories

Sprinkled tales in the twilight air,
Whiskers tickling, oh do beware!
Nostalgia sings in a giddy tone,
As each soft thread tells stories grown.

Mismatched buttons and tangled yarn,
Each quirky piece brings a smile, not scorn.
Floating in laughter, they gather near,
A whimsical quilt, stitched with cheer.

Illuminated Blooms of Potential

Petals burst with a giggling spree,
Colors dance as bright as can be.
Bouncing light on the playful ground,
In this garden, joy knows no bound.

Bees in tuxedos, buzzing in glee,
Honey-filled whispers of possibility.
Each bloom a chuckle, a tiptoe delight,
In a vibrant world, the future's so bright.

Rhythms of the Divine Weave

A jolly tapestry swings in time,
With knitted punchlines that perfectly rhyme.
Twists and shouts, in sync with the beat,
This joyous dance will sweep you off your feet.

Each thread a story, each knot a laugh,
In the melody of patterns, we find our path.
Bouncing in stitches, oh what a treat,
In the divine weave, the rhythm's so sweet.

Phantoms in the Fabric

In shadows where the threads entwine,
The ghosts of stitches sip on wine.
They dance in patterns quite absurd,
While mocking every spoken word.

A seam that grins, a hem that giggles,
Buttons prance and play hop-skiddles.
Each flap and fold a prankster's jest,
Fabric's funhouse, a silly fest.

Lacework of Whispered Promises

Promises draped like moths at night,
Whispers hiding just out of sight.
A thread of mischief, a playful tease,
Stitched with chuckles, aiming to please.

Giggling seams in a wild ballet,
Naughty words in a woven display.
Every loop's a tale to tell,
In this fabric realm, we dance and yell!

Celestial Patterns Against the Sky

Stars strut in their twinkling shoes,
Dancing amid the cosmic blues.
Comets swoosh with a laugh and a twirl,
While planets spin in a fabric whirl.

Galaxies spin their silly yarns,
Crafting jokes with their flaring charms.
The universe chuckles at its grand scheme,
We're all just threads in one big dream!

Glancing Light Through Elegance

Dainty threads that wink and shine,
A fashion faux pas, oh so divine.
Bowing lights in a playful show,
Tickling elegance, to and fro.

Chiffon giggles, silk lets out sighs,
As glances shimmer with cheeky lies.
In a room of whispers, they tease and flaunt,
Making fun of all who dare to haunt.

Celestial Tapestry of Dreams

In a web of stars, I tripped on a beam,
Fell into a swirling, giggling dream.
Bouncing on clouds made of cream and spunk,
With puzzled moonbeams, my silliness junk.

Jupiter winked with a playful glare,
While Saturn tossed rings like a fairground chair.
I danced with comets in sneakers so bright,
Chasing the laughter that shimmered at night.

Shimmering Secrets of the Weave

A hamster in space wore a shiny bow tie,
With secretive giggles, he learned how to fly.
Twirling through nebulae, making a brand,
He spun tales of mischief on shimmering strands.

Whispers of stardust tickled my ear,
As silly old planets spun faster in cheer.
Each twinkling glitter held hints of delight,
In the tapestry woven from humor and light.

Dances in Hallowed Radiance

The sun wore a tutu, all bright and bold,
While the moon, in a beret, shared stories untold.
Planets with maracas shook up the night,
As galaxies jived, what a fun little sight!

In fields of soft starlight, I lost my shoe,
Chasing a shadow that tickled me too.
With each twirl and giggle, my worries took flight,
In sacred hallowed halls of a whimsical night.

Threads of Gold in Soft Embrace

A squirrel donned shades, took a dip in the stream,
While turtles debated the best chocolate dream.
In the warmth of the sunset, their laughter would flow,
As fireflies painted the world with a glow.

We danced in the whispers of evening's delight,
With socks on our heads, oh, what a sight!
The fabric of joy stitched with giggles and glee,
In a world spun from laughter, just silly and free.

Ethereal Cradles of Time

In a world where socks go missing,
The clocks tick backward, quite dismissing.
A cat sits sipping tea, so refined,
While I search for my left shoes, unaligned.

Butterflies with hats float in the breeze,
Telling jokes to the dandelions with ease.
I wonder if they snicker at my plight,
As I trip over my thoughts in the night.

Enchanted Silhouettes of Dawn

The roosters crow in funny rhyme,
While I giggle at the clock's wrong time.
A rabbit in slippers hops down the street,
Delivering breakfast that's hard to beat.

Gnomes play chess with starry skies,
Counting clouds as they strategize.
Who knew dawn could laugh so loud?
With shadows dancing, all around.

Glimmering Hues, Endless Possibilities

Crayons scribble stories untold,
As the silly sun drops, bright and bold.
Pineapple hats on penguins parade,
While marshmallow clouds join in the charade.

Rainbows twist into noodle shapes,
Mermaids leap with silly scrapes.
Every color laughs and plays,
In a world where silliness always stays.

The Fabric of Forgotten Dreams

In a closet where wishes collect dust,
A sock puppet recites poems, as it must.
With cereal bowls on its head so grand,
    It tells tales of a far-off land.

Umbrellas bloom like flowers in May,
As umbrellas dance the cha-cha sway.
  I trip and tumble, what a sight,
  In a carnival of dreams tonight.

Fading Patterns at the Edge of Light

In twilight's glow, patterns dance,
A blur of joy, some clumsy prance.
They zig and zag, in silly style,
While shadows giggle, all the while.

Beneath the glow, they twist and twine,
Like noodles tossed in broth divine.
The evening's snack, a sight to see,
A tapestry made just for me.

Old jokes unwind, they flutter free,
Caught in the weave of memory.
Laughter threads the air with grace,
And humor wraps us in its embrace.

The fading hues, they do confound,
As giggles echo all around.
In patterns lost, we find the fun,
A tapestry spun for everyone.

The Touch of Graceful Formation

With whims and fancies taking flight,
A ticklish breeze, a sheer delight.
Each twist and turn, a playful game,
An artful touch, no two the same.

Wobbly shapes and jiggly lines,
Like festive dance of silly vines.
They sway about, with such a flair,
Making fun of who might care.

Giggling echoes from afar,
As whimsy shapes a shining star.
The slippery folds, they laugh and prance,
Inviting all to join the dance.

In bounding leaps, they merry-go,
Creating joy where'er they flow.
Through graceful skips, we find our way,
In a giggle-fest, we wish to stay.

Mystical Crevices of Shimmering Gold

In corners rich, a shine unfolds,
Where secrets hide and laughter scolds.
The nooks and crannies whisper sweet,
In gleeful tones, they skip and greet.

A puddle glints, a pie on high,
With dreams as fresh as pumpkin pie.
The shimmer sings a silly tune,
That tickles rays of the warm moon.

Through gilded cracks where light can peek,
The shadows play a game of sneak.
A sassy smile beneath the glow,
Makes every crevice laugh and grow.

With sparkles trailing like confetti,
Each little joke lands soft and heavy.
Together we find gold in jest,
In mystic hugs, we feel the zest.

Dappled Dreams in Ethereal Tones

In playful shades where giggles weave,
A dappled quilt, how we believe!
Soft whispers float on gentle breeze,
While dreams parade with playful tease.

The shimmering hues, they jump and soar,
In merry shapes, they want some more.
With jokester's charm, they start to twirl,
As silly rhythms make us whirl.

Through eccentric paths of colored fun,
The tones collide, a quirky run.
In every brush, a jest appears,
A party waiting through the years.

As echoes ripple, laughter rings,
Dappled dreams share all their things.
In lunacy's warm, vibrant embrace,
We find our joy, our funny place.

Lace-Like Echoes of Serenity

In a world of tangled threads,
Where socks and mittens always fled.
A needle pricks at my grand design,
With giggles weaving in every line.

Hooks and yarn dance at my feet,
A tangle of colors, oh what a feat!
Each stitch creates a little cheer,
While kittens nap without a fear.

My blanket's a monster, all fluffy and wide,
With a polka-dot pattern that took quite a ride.
It waved at the mailman, almost a flight,
Who laughed at my madness, what a silly sight!

So here I sit, in my whimsical nook,
With threads and chuckles, just take a look!
Each loop a laugh, each slip a jest,
In this knitted kingdom, I am truly blessed.

Infinite Stitches of Harmonics

With hooks that jingle, I weave and spin,
In a melody of yarn, let the fun begin!
Each stitch a note in my playful song,
And who knew crafting could feel so strong?

I tangled my scarf with a dash of flair,
An accidental knot that became a pair!
With frills and curls, it went awry,
Like a disco party, oh my oh my!

Purling and knitting, I set off to play,
Where every mistake leads me further astray.
It wobbles and giggles like on a breeze,
Making my craft time feel like a tease.

But deep down, in each playful twist,
Is a melody crafted that can't be missed.
So here's to the joy in what we create,
Embrace the chaos, it's never too late!

Woven Gleams of Hope

In a loom of laughter, I spin my dreams,
With threads of sunshine and cheerful beams.
A fabric of wishes, bright and surreal,
Each color a giggle, each touch a squeal.

My creations droop like a floppy hat,
What began as a scarf just looks like a cat!
It zooms and flops like a happy balloon,
Bringing charm and laughter all afternoon.

With every loop, a spark of delight,
It sways with abandon, oh what a sight!
It couldn't hold back all its great glee,
For what is crafting, if not to be free?

So gather your bits and bobs with care,
For humor and crafting go quite well, I swear!
In each tiny stitch, there's a joke to behold,
Woven in joy, in colors untold.

Threads of Solitude Under Brightness

Alone in my corner, I quietly giggle,
When tangled creations make me wiggle.
A ball of yarn, my long-lost friend,
With puns and purls, the fun never ends.

I planned to create a grand, cozy throw,
But it turned out to be more of a glow!
With mismatched squares and stripes so bold,
A masterpiece bright, or so I'm told.

My feline connoisseur inspects with a glare,
As my project becomes a snug little chair.
Each twist of fabric a jest to unveil,
In this realm of chaos, I shall prevail!

So let's all embrace our quirky creations,
With threads of laughter in wild foundations.
In this woven oddity, let joy be the guide,
For the heart is a canvas, with smiles as its pride.

Light's Embrace in Filigree

A dance of shadows on the floor,
They twirl and shimmy, who needs more?
Each ray a partner, bold and bright,
In silly steps, they take their flight.

Threads of humor, woven keen,
With every giggle, a new scene.
The sun wears shades, the moon a grin,
As beams poke fun and play to win.

Fanciful birds make jesters sing,
While petals chuckle in the spring.
Winking light, like a playful sprite,
Brings joy amidst the fading night.

In this realm, the bright does tease,
Catching laughter on the breeze.
So join the jest, don't miss the show,
In cobwebs spun with joyous glow.

Soft Echoes of Silver and Gold

Whispers shimmer in golden gleam,
As shadows giggle in the beam.
A silver cat with a shiny coat,
Announces laughter, just like a note.

The sun's a jester, bright and spry,
Telling tales that seem to fly.
While sparrows chirp a tune so sweet,
To each soft echo, they tap their feet.

Glints of mirth in every nook,
As giggles splash and laughter crook.
The world is brighter, can't you see?
In this parade of jest and glee.

Where silver threads and gold entwine,
A tapestry of fun, divine.
So sip the day like sweetened tea,
And dance along with glee, carefree.

Fragments of Radiance in Threads

Bits of sparkle, a playful jest,
Fractured beams, they feel so blessed.
A rainbow's giggle, what a sight,
In threads of joy, heaven takes flight.

Luminous patches play hide and seek,
With winks and nudges, oh-so-bleak.
Each shimmer whispers, "Guess my game!"
As morning stretches, calling their names.

Here comes the sparkle, ready to go,
Joking about in a brilliant show.
As shadows giggle in bright parade,
Creating laughter that will not fade.

The dance goes on, a merry spree,
In fragments woven, wild and free.
So hold your smile and take a chance,
Join the radiance in this dance.

Twilight's Gossamer Embrace

Under the glow of twilight's tease,
A canvas painted with cheeky breezes.
The stars wear hats, all sequined bright,
As giggles bubble up in the night.

Spiders spin webs of shiny charm,
They laugh and prance, causing no harm.
While foxes leap, in the fading glow,
Each step is light, each jest a show.

The moon, a jolly old fellow,
Winks at the world, feeling mellow.
His giggles spread through tree and flower,
Twilight's beauty holds a funny power.

Wrap yourself in this whimsical dream,
Where laughter flows like a bubbly stream.
In gossamer threads, the night declares,
Joy's hidden here, if only one dares.

Interlaced Dreams and Daylight

In a world of tangled threads,
The sun spills joys like lemon spreads.
A sock that dances on its own,
Who knew the gnomes had seeds to sown?

Twisted tales in morning's glee,
Antics of the cat and me.
The toaster jumps, a breakfast show,
With pop-up toast, oh what a glow!

Sleepy hats on wrinkled heads,
Chasing ducks in rainbow beds.
The milk jug wears a funny grin,
While cereal's swirling with a spin!

In dreams where everything's askew,
I play hopscotch on the blue.
A frolic through these woven beams,
While giggling softly through my dreams.

A Silken Pathway to Serenity

A ribbon trails through cotton skies,
Where peanut butter laughs and flies.
The garden gnome does jazz ballet,
While squirrels cheer his grand display.

A pathway made of candy canes,
Where ginger snaps sing silly refrains.
Fluffy clouds in cotton candy,
Bringing joy, oh isn't that dandy?

In the land of twinkly stars,
Socks play tag, and we drive cars.
The fireplace tells a tale of cheese,
As giggles dance upon the breeze.

With every hop and silly slide,
The world becomes a playful ride.
In every twist of fate and fun,
A silken path for everyone.

The Twilights of Textured Heart

In the twilight where mischief weaves,
A cookie jar that giggles and leaves.
The teddy bears have quite the chat,
While wearing hats too big for that!

A textured heart that skips a beat,
With marshmallow shoes on little feet.
They dance and prance with every sigh,
While jellybeans bounce to the sky.

Pumpkin pie wears a smirk so wide,
As the oranges take a wobbly ride.
In this land of sweet parade,
Textures twist in a playful charade.

So here we stand, with laughter near,
Among the snacks, we have no fear.
The twilight hugs us, warm and true,
In a hug made of sparkles too.

Velvet Echoes of a Distant Dawn

A velvet dawn whispers softly sweet,
Tickling toes with eager greet.
Waffle slippers skip with glee,
As squirrels plot an evening spree.

The echoes here are silly sounds,
With cocoa swirls and jelly bounds.
A sandwich sings a hearty song,
As pickles jump and dance along.

Each brush of morning paints the scene,
Where corny jokes reign supreme.
The clock ticks off with cheeky chime,
While breakfast asks for extra thyme.

In velvet hues, we laugh and play,
As echoes charm the break of day.
Together spun, we strut and sway,
For every dawn brings jokes to stay.

Veiled in Gilded Hours

In a world that winks and twirls,
Where whispers tickle like a feather,
A dance of shadows swirls,
Creating mishaps we tether.

With a hop, a skip, a giggle,
As thoughts twist and twine in jest,
The clock ticks and we wriggle,
Chasing time like a silly quest.

A tangled yarn of jest and cheer,
We weave our tales without a care,
Entwined with laughter drawing near,
A fabric rich, beyond compare.

In shimmering hues of playful grace,
We paint our dreams, light-heartedly,
For in this whimsical embrace,
We find our joy, so happily.

Fluttering Light Beneath a Silk Canopy

Beneath the shade where giggles sway,
A fluttering breeze plays peek-a-boo,
With shadows that chase and sway,
Like butterflies that love to construe.

A squabble of sprites in endless flight,
With antics that lift spirits high,
They tickle the sun to giggle bright,
As clouds parade by, oh my!

In this woven world of playful strains,
A patchwork quilt of jest and cheer,
Where even the raindrops join in refrains,
Laughter sparkles, warm and clear.

So let's dance beneath this quilt so wide,
Twisting and turning under the sun,
In a swirling, skipping, playful ride,
Together, until the day is done.

Celestial Artistry of the Invisible

In the theater where stars prance,
A cosmic jest unfolds so bright,
Screening the universe's chance,
We twirl with glee in the night.

With twinkling eyes and glowing grins,
The moon winks at our retreat,
Creating mischief where joy begins,
A secret game that's quite sweet.

Invisible threads of laughter flow,
Binding us to the cosmic play,
In orbits where night-time breezes blow,
We find our giggles on display.

So let's frolic in this starry jest,
Among the wonders of the spree,
Where whimsy guides our restless quest,
And dreams dance wild and free.

The Quiet Symphony of Evening's Glow

As daylight bows to twilight's craze,
A hush drapes over the end of day,
With whispers that dance in a playful maze,
Inviting shadows in their ballet.

The crickets chirp a cheeky tune,
While fireflies flicker like wayward stars,
In this gentle gloaming, a playful boon,
A canvas of humor, without any bars.

In this serene, yet lively show,
Each chuckle weaves the night anew,
Under the glow, where feelings flow,
We gather mirth in shades of blue.

So let the evening unfold its schemes,
With laughter echoing soft and light,
For in this symphony of dreams,
Joy dances freely into the night.

Ethereal Patterns in Twilight

In twilight's cloak, so sheer and bright,
People trip on ghosts of white.
They dance and twirl, a sight to see,
Laughing hard, but who's that bee?

With stitches done in mismatched thread,
They wove a tale with visions spread.
Yet spools went flying, oh what a show,
Who knew that crafting could throw such a glow?

Cascading colors, spirals in the air,
A kitten jumps into this fair.
But tangled up, she feigns surprise,
Wrapped in magic, whining ties.

So grab a friend and take a seat,
Join the fun, embrace the heat.
For in this world of thread and cheer,
We'll bask in joy, we'll shed a tear.

Glimmers in the Woven Breeze

Breezy whispers, how they sway,
A tapestry tries to stray.
Chasing fireflies on the run,
Sorry, they're just here for fun.

A weaver with a quirky grin,
Stitches dance; just where to begin?
With braids that twist, and curls that fry,
The cats are laughing, oh me, oh my!

Gather friends for a picnic feast,
On fabric bright, we're truly pleased.
But watch your drink, oh what a fright,
That ant is claiming it tonight!

So let's toss some feathers in the air,
Embrace the chaos, we don't care!
For in this funny textile game,
Life is a riot with no one to blame.

A Tangle of Glows and Hues

A mess of colors, what a sight,
The rainbow's lost its way tonight.
With twisted threads and giggles loud,
Please, become a fabric crowd!

In the garden with the daisies bright,
A spinning wheel goes left and right.
Caught with a tickle, don't you see?
The plants just joined, oh woe is me!

Patterns fly, like geese on parade,
Each step they take turns into jade.
But turtles join, they're taking bets,
On who will win, the laughter's set.

So share a tale, make it a yarn,
Together we'll create some charm.
In this wacky world of hues,
No rules to guide—all fun ensues!

The Touch of Morning's Embrace

As morning winks, a playful tease,
A blanket spread from trees to knees.
We stretch and yawn, our eyes aglow,
With pancakes leaping, don't they know?

Sunbeams bounce on crafty threads,
While squirrels weave their cozy beds.
With laughter ringing through the park,
A chase ensues, igniting spark!

"Catch that donut!" someone shouts,
Amidst the chaos, joy abounds.
Woven tales and giggles bright,
Together we glow, with pure delight.

So raise a mug to mornings sweet,
For friendship makes this life complete.
In this dance of warmth and grace,
Each moment glimmers—oh, what a place!

The Glow of Woven Secrets

In a tapestry of giggles, they weave,
Secrets dance like dust in the eve.
Each thread a story, a whimsy delight,
Twisting and spinning, they catch the night.

With knots of laughter, they bungle and play,
Hiding mischief in patterns so gay.
A stitch in time saves moments of cheer,
As yarns unravel, the jokes appear.

All woven wonders, so silly and bright,
A fabric of joy, a marvelous sight.
In the glow of their crafting, they find a spark,
For threads of the day weave tales in the dark.

So let's celebrate the foolish and fun,
With garments of giggles that can never be done.
In this vibrant quilt, we dance and delight,
Woven secrets emerge in the softest night.

Dappled Illusions of the Morning

Sunrise whispers in cheeky tones,
Paints the world with mishaps and moans.
Coffee spills on the new white sheet,
Morning mischief, a comical feat.

Shadows play hopscotch on the floor,
Tripping over the cat, who wants more.
Roosters bragging, all in a chase,
Dappled dreams shattered, a merry disgrace.

With every giggle, the day unfolds,
Best-laid plans turn to comical gold.
Pajamas peek like a fashion dare,
Illusions of morning float in the air.

So rise and embrace this whimsical feel,
Life's playful banter, a delightful reel.
In dappled hues, we'll dance and clink,
Finding joy's fabric in every wink.

Wisping Veils of Radiance

A gentle breeze teases wayside dreams,
Where shadows shift in the sun's playful beams.
Veils of hilarity brush past our face,
Flirting with bright joy, a giggling chase.

Socks mismatched in a splendid parade,
Each step a bounce, in silly charade.
Fluffy clouds whisper notes of the day,
As we twirl round in this light-hearted play.

The sun winks at the jester's cap,
In the tapestry of laughter, we take a nap.
Radiance flickers, with each silly glance,
In wisping veils, we twirl and dance.

So hold fast to chuckles, let giggles reign,
In this glowing maze, we'll never complain.
For every shimmer holds secrets so grand,
Wrapped in the warmth of our whimsical band.

The Embrace of Soft Shadows

Under the arches where whispers reside,
Soft shadows stretch, in laughter they hide.
With giggles that bounce off the cobblestone,
Every nook and cranny feels just like home.

A jigsaw puzzle of sunlight and grins,
Playing peek-a-boo, where the morning begins.
Laughter spills over the edges of time,
In playful embrace, life dances in rhyme.

Old chairs creak with stories well spun,
In the cozy corners, the banter's begun.
Thoughts rattle on like wind chimes out loud,
As shadows play tricks, all lightheartedly proud.

In a flutter of whimsy, our hearts take flight,
Finding joy in the mundane, a pure delight.
So let's revel in shadows, soft and absurd,
Where laughter's the magic, and happiness inferred.

Woven Reflections in Every Tear

In a puddle of giggles, I see,
Each drop dances, as if it's free.
Stitched together by rumpled dreams,
Sewing joy as laughter beams.

A tangle of thoughts, both mad and bright,
Stitching together day and night.
In threads of chaos, we find our play,
A tapestry woven in a quirky way.

Graced by Morning's Soft Gesture

Awake with the sun's gentle poke,
Chasing shadows like a silly joke.
The coffee pot sings, oh what a treat,
Morning's brew can't be beat!

A sock thrown high, lands on my head,
With breakfast crumbles, I'm half-fed.
Butterflies flit in bright ballet,
As giggles chase the grumpies away.

Luminous Paths on a Dreamer's Canvas

Doodles of hopes and wishes collide,
A colorful mess, I cannot hide.
Crayons argue, each wants to win,
In this race of colors, let's begin!

With splatters and smudges, joy does bloom,
As laughter erupts from each little room.
A masterpiece born from a silly thought,
In this wacky world, I gleefully trot.

Interwoven Time and Day

Tick-tock goes the silly clock,
Wrinkles appear with each fun shock.
Time hops around like a playful pup,
In this wild dance, we can't give up!

Threads of moments weave and roam,
Creating chaos in every home.
With giggles stitched into the fray,
We embrace the quirks of each bright day.

Twinkling Threads in Twilight

In twilight's glow, the threads unwind,
A playful dance, they're hard to find.
Tangles make a mess, oh what a sight,
Who knew sewing could turn into a fight?

Stitches giggle, prancing so free,
One says, 'Hey, don't pull on me!'
As needles laugh at errors made,
A fabric circus in which we wade.

Patterns swirl, and stripes collide,
'Oops!' cries one in a fabric slide.
A patchwork puzzle with mismatched glee,
Every stitch just cracks up, you see!

Twilight fades, but the laughter remains,
With threads and giggles, it's never mundane.
In the quiet night, we'll thread again,
For humor lingers, that's our true gain.

Ethereal Embrace of Dawn

Morning breaks with threads so bright,
Silk and cotton, oh what a sight!
Fabric tussles in the sun's warm glow,
One sock whispers, 'Where'd you go?'

A button rolls, what a silly game,
Sewing needles dance, they'll take the blame.
Twisted seams laugh and play,
'Who knew we'd have fun this way?'

Dawn's embrace tickles the cloth,
Wandering threads, should we be sloth?
We tripped and slipped, that's how it goes,
In the morning light, anything shows!

With stitches that waltz and fibers that giggle,
Every morning begins with a jiggle.
So grab your thread and sew with cheer,
For the day's bright antics are finally here!

Light's Gentle Touch on Fabric

The fabric whispers under the sun,
Ticklish fibers, oh what fun!
A stray thread wiggles, feeling bright,
Saying, 'I'm ready for a silly flight!'

Strands intertwine in a comical way,
Who knew fabric yearned to play?
A quilt puffs up with a hearty laugh,
As threads form lines in a quirky graph.

Every patch has stories to tell,
Of knitting mishaps and sewing as well.
With a wink and a fold, they charm us all,
In this jumbled fabric, we have a ball.

Letting go of order, they embrace the fun,
In a colorful world, together they run.
It's just a weave of light, you see,
Where humor and thread dance in unity!

Sunbeams Caught in Tangles

Sunbeams weave through a fabric maze,
Catching fibers in a golden blaze.
'Oh no!' squeaks a thread, 'I'm stuck!'
Laughter erupts, oh what luck!

Colors swirl in a crazy array,
Who knew fabrics would have their day?
A patch fell down with a happy squeal,
'Get the camera, this is a steal!'

Strings are knotted in a joyful way,
Each loop a reason to dance and sway.
Draped in sunlight, with giggles galore,
What a sight, we simply adore!

As shadows stretch and evening looms,
Our carousel spins in blushing blooms.
With tangled threads, we find delight,
In this merry dance till the end of night.

Shadows Woven in Silk

In seams of shadows, I do trip,
A fabric blunder as I slip.
With threads that tease, they dance and play,
Making me laugh, what a funny fray!

A curtain's wink, a sly little game,
Causing my heart to burst into flame.
All those loops, they tease my feet,
I swear, they're out for a giggle feat!

Oh, patterns tease like playful mice,
They twist and turn, oh, isn't that nice?
A thread unspooled, what a sight!
I tumble down, just feeling light!

So here's to fabric, jokes on the side,
Each woven fumble, a joyful ride.
In this funny realm of soft and sleek,
I'll embrace the laugh each time I peek!

Sunlit Patterns on the Floor

Sunbeams shimmy, a floor of cheer,
Dancing in circles, I jump in here!
With every shadow, a funny surprise,
Are those my feet or giant flies?

Twirling threads of sunshine gleam,
They pull me in, oh what a dream!
I skip and slide, with grace I implore,
Just try not to trip, can't take it anymore!

In this patchwork of giggles and tones,
The floor's a canvas of silly bones.
Each footprint left, a burst of delight,
Sunlit laughter, oh, what a sight!

So let the patterns wrap me tight,
Every chuckle a sweet respite.
With sunlit joy, I'll dance once more,
Forever caught on this playful floor!

Filigree Dreams at Dusk

As daylight fades, I chase a whim,
In dreams of filigree, laughter's brim.
Frills and curls begin to bloom,
With jokes that fill this twilight room!

Woven tales of night unfold,
Where mischief hides, and antics bold.
The dusk unravels, I can't resist,
What pranks await in this gentle mist?

With threads of twilight, my thoughts collide,
A tapestry of grins where giggles reside.
Every stitch holds a secret jest,
In this dream realm, we laugh the best!

So let the night weave its magic, all right?
Each wink and nod make my heart feel light.
In filigree dreams, I'll dance and sway,
Sharing chuckles till the break of day!

Gossamer Hues of Morning

In gossamer hues, the dawn arrives,
With playful whispers and winking jives.
A thread of gold, a shimmer here,
Oh look! A sleepy bear, with morning cheer!

Sunrise tickles, the day begins,
With dodging shadows and silly spins.
I fumble forward, a yawn escapes,
Pretending I'm an owl, with silly shapes!

Breezes flutter, the curtains sway,
Each twist and turn, oh, what a play!
With giggles woven between each beam,
A fun-filled morning, not as it seems!

So here's to hours of bright delight,
When gossamer hues bring laughter's light.
In the dance of dawn, let joy take flight,
With every chuckle, the day feels right!

The Embrace of Dappled Patterns

In a world of polka dots,
A raccoon in the park dances a lot.
He stumbles in stripes, trips on a line,
Yet smiles wide, feeling just fine.

With plaid squirrels and checked trees,
The wind whispers jokes, as sweet as a breeze.
Silk worms giggle, their thread-making art,
As the trees laugh loudly, keeping the heart.

Oh, tangled up in colors that clash,
Cheerful chaos, a very fine mash.
Dancing in circles, around and around,
Nature's odd patterns, the joy that we found.

So twirl with the twists and sway with the bends,
In a world where a fabric like laughter transcends.
It's a patchwork of whimsy, a joyful delight,
In this playful embrace, we're lost in the night.

Enchanted Woven Threads

Threads of fortune, spun so bright,
A spider fell down, what a silly sight!
He wove a web with amusing flair,
Cat got entangled? Oh, a comedic scare!

Strands of dreams in a knitted mess,
A grandma's blanket, but who can guess?
The dog's on the couch, wrapped in soft hue,
Trying to fit in – well, good luck to you!

In a tapestry, laughter we sew,
Whimsical patterns begin to grow.
A unicorn prances, then trips on its tail,
In the land of yarn, even giants can fail.

So heed this tale of fabric and cheer,
When stitches go wild, embrace all the dear.
Life is a quilt, with patches and grooves,
Filled with the moments that dance and that move.

Hues of Dawn and Dusk

Morning paints the sky a glow,
But breakfast spills? Oh, what a show!
Coffee slides down the table's side,
The cereal swims, gives the milk a ride.

Colors collide, in a breakfast mess,
Eggs dance together, we wish them success.
Sunlight giggles, as shadows creep,
Who will clean up? Not us, we'll just leap!

As daylight fades, the colors twirl,
A disco party for each sun-swirled pearl.
The moon juggles stars, what a foolish delight,
Even the owls dance, in the cloak of night.

So gather the hues, let laughter persist,
Nature's own palette, add flair to the list.
With each dawn and dusk, let the whimsy ignite,
In this colorful frolic, we'll live to shine bright.

The Entwined Glow of Memories

In a box of trinkets, memories gleam,
A rubber duck sings out, 'Life's but a dream!'
Old photos stick together like glue,
Who knew Aunt Edna had a skateboard crew?

A bubblegum bracelet, oh what a find,
The stories it holds might boggle the mind.
A yo-yo flips back, with a wink and a spin,
Echoes of laughter, where do we begin?

The tangled cords, of laughter and cheer,
Dance through the stories we hold so dear.
Each little knickknack, a tale to unfold,
In the treasure of moments, our hearts are consoled.

So cherish the spark of the things that we keep,
In this jumbled voyage, through memories deep.
For each quirky treasure, in colors so bright,
Divines the darkness, as we embrace the light.

The Caress of Daybreak's Weave

Morning's fingers tickle the cheek,
A dance of shadows starts to peek.
Frogs in pajamas sing their tune,
While cats play chess with a bright balloon.

Roosters strut, adorned in flair,
Chasing sunshine with utmost care.
Socks that don't match, oh what a sight,
In this grand ballet of morning light.

Dewdrops giggle on grass blades fair,
Grasshoppers leap with the utmost flair.
A squirrel slips, oh what a flop,
As daybreak whispers, "Do not stop!"

So we toast to the start of day,
In the bizarre, we find our play.
With each silly twist, the world gleams bright,
As chuckles bloom in morning's light.

Silken Trails of Radiant Paths

At the fair, the banners swoosh,
While puppies prance and a goose goes 'whoosh'.
Cotton candy clouds puff up high,
As ticklish fancies flutter and fly.

The clown's shoes squeak with flair and charm,
While juggling pies without alarm.
Children giggle, sparks in their eyes,
As sprinkles tumble from candy skies.

A raccoon dons a tiny bow,
As cotton candy steals the show.
Oh, the wonders on this crazy lane,
Where joy is sprinkled like summer rain.

With cotton dreams, we laugh and spin,
In this playful world, let fun begin.
Through trails of whimsical, we'll glide,
Sharing giggles as our hearts collide.

Threads of Golden Whisper

In a field of sneaky flowers bright,
Bees in sunglasses enjoy their flight.
A butterfly slips on its own groove,
As petals tango in a gentle move.

Breezes laugh, a gentle tease,
While daisies gossip under trees.
A sunflower winks with a golden grin,
As daisies debate who'll wear the win.

Ants march on, a little parade,
While ladybugs sing in a playful serenade.
The grasshoppers join with a leap and hop,
In nature's laugh, we will never stop.

So come, let's frolic in fields so grand,
With whispers of joy at our command.
As golden moments slip and sway,
We'll giggle through this lively day.

Echoes of Sunlit Fantasies

A sunbeam tickles the sleepy trees,
While rabbits dance like they're on a spree.
Frolicking squirrels play hide and seek,
In a game of shadows, they mysteriously peek.

Clouds wear smiles, fluffy and white,
As the world laughs in pure delight.
Grass blades become a giggling stage,
In this playful book, we start a new page.

A rubber chicken joins the fun,
As laughter sparkles like dew at dawn.
Colorful dreams drape every scene,
In the silly tales where we've all been.

So let's chase echoes, wild and sweet,
With every chuckle, our hearts repeat.
In sun-kissed moments, let's take flight,
In the magic of this merry light.

The Nature of Delicate Enchantment

In a world of frills and threads,
Dancing socks have silly heads.
A blouse that twirls in joyful glee,
Giggles float like honeybee.

Ribbons tangled in a chase,
A scarf that sneezes in the face.
Whispers from a shimmery mask,
Lurking in a playful task.

To spin us in a tangled bite,
With petticoats and sprightly light.
A jacket wears a tiny frog,
While socks are lost in playful fog.

Frolicsome fabrics, jolly hues,
A tunic that sings silly blues.
In this realm where laughter meets,
We twirl in fineries and sweets.

Translucent Realities

A curtain flutters with a grin,
Socks debate on who will win.
To peek or not, that is the play,
Where shadows dance and blithely sway.

See-through shirts share funny things,
About the joy that laughter brings.
A light breeze whispers winks and sighs,
While rolls of fabric tell no lies.

Translucent tunics hold a secret,
The cats believe they can keep it.
While jumpers boast of bold confessions,
Knitting tales of wild obsessions.

Invisible threads that tie us tight,
In the clumsiness of morning light.
So let's embrace this charming scare,
In every stitch, we have a flair.

Weaving Shadows into Comfort

In shadows where the blankets fold,
A sweater tells a tale of gold.
With comfy hugs and teasing light,
A snuggle zone for playful night.

The throw pillows join in a fight,
Over who gets the cozy right.
With giggles woven through each seam,
In the fabric, we all dream.

The curtains mock the sneaky sun,
While slippers boast they're more than fun.
With yarn that dances in delight,
Beneath a starry, cozy sight.

So gather 'round the playful fades,
In comfy zones where love cascades.
For every shadow holds a spark,
In this embrace, let's leave our mark.

Golden Threads of Memory

In wardrobes where old garments sleep,
Golden threads begin to creep.
Reminders of a wild parade,
Where silly dances were displayed.

With polka dots and stripes so bold,
Each fabric whispers tales of old.
The time socks formed a areal band,
And all the laughter close at hand.

A hat that tips with grand finesse,
Recalls the fun in every dress.
While every thread weaves in a grin,
Memories swirling, letting us in.

So stitch by stitch, we'll find our way,
Through tapestries of joy at play.
With every fabric that we save,
We craft the laughter that we crave.

Threads of Radiance

A stitch in time saves nine, or so they say,
But I lost count while sewing all day.
Thread tangles like cats in a playful fight,
Yet the colors mix, oh what a sight!

My needle dances with a life of its own,
Each pull and tug, a melodious tone.
I swear it giggles with every twist,
As patterns emerge, I can't resist!

Fabric swirls and takes flight,
Turning my room into a wild sight.
A headdress of buttons and ribbons so grand,
I'm now the queen of a magic land!

In this chaotic haven, joy takes a stand,
As fabric friends gather hand in hand.
So join the fun, don't you be shy,
Let's sew up some laughter that reaches the sky!

Whispered Embers in Silk

A patchwork quilt of quirky delight,
Each square tells tales that tickle the night.
In corners, I find a sock that's long gone,
A missing shoe, did it steal off with dawn?

The colors clash, like socks in the wash,
Pastel pink paired with neon green posh.
Yet laughter erupts at this riotous flair,
Even fabric groans in a stylish despair!

Slips of silk in a frisky ballet,
Twist and twirl while the thread leads the way.
Noble fabrics, what tales you would weave,
If only you spoke, oh, how we'd believe!

As embers flicker, secrets unfold,
Each fold contains a fun story told.
Stitching a zany life, don't you agree?
A blanket of dreams, come dance here with me!

Gossamer Dreams Under the Moon

Under the stars, my fabric takes flight,
Dancing and swirling, what a funny sight!
A ghost made of tulle, with a wink and a grin,
Whispers secrets of the fabric within.

Threads so fine glide like they're on air,
Over my shoulders as if they do care.
With laughter erupting, they twirl 'round my head,
Who knew that crafting could lead to such dread?

Glittery patches in a dreamlike ballet,
Every snip a surprise, oh what a display!
Even the bobbin seems ready to play,
As my sewing machine takes me far away.

In the glow of the moon, mishaps abound,
But joy leads the way, so freely unbound.
So come share a laugh in this whimsical room,
Embracing each moment, let's make the gloom bloom!

Shimmers through Heirloom Weaves

In grandma's attic, I find treasures untold,
A tapestry of memories that never grow old.
A shirt that still laughs at its faded design,
An old patch from a party, where I crossed the line!

Threads shimmer softly like fireflies bright,
Winking at mischief before taking flight.
I stitch and I snip, it's a comical scene,
With each snappy move, I embrace the routine!

A jacket fits oddly, but laughter ignites,
As I strut down the hall with a mix of delight.
Oh, look at the pattern that clashed with the day,
Who knew my wardrobe would lead me to play?

In these heirloom weaves, stories grow bold,
Woven together, both young and old.
So let's share a giggle, a wink, and a cheer,
In this fabric-filled world, we've nothing to fear!

The Delicate Dance of Daybreak

In morning's blush, the curtains sway,
Like dancers prancing, come what may.
A twist, a turn, they steal the show,
Who knew the dawn had such a glow?

With breakfast waits a frothy spill,
A coffee splash—what a thrill!
The sunlight giggles, streaks its rays,
While toast does a wobbly ballet.

The socks are mismatched, out of sight,
A playful fight with morning light.
Awake, the world begins to laugh,
As shadows dance upon the path.

In this soft glow, all things are bright,
A funny tale of day and night.
The morning's here, so grab your hat,
Embrace the silliness of that!

Frail Fabrics of a New Sun

The sun sneaks up in softest hues,
Wearing pajamas, with mismatched shoes.
It pokes its head to see the grin,
Of chirpy birds, a playful din.

Gentle whispers rustle through trees,
Like giggles caught in fluttering breeze.
Each petal opens, yawns in delight,
As if saying, 'Oh, what a sight!'

The sun spills coffee on the sky,
While the clouds lazily drift by.
A sprinkle of cheer, a dash of fun,
A comic skit has just begun.

In this funny patchwork we reside,
Where nature's quirks can't help but guide.
So sip your joy and dance along,
With frail fibers to make you strong!

Radiance in the Weft

Threads of sunshine weave the day,
In a tapestry of light ballet.
A flicker here, a sparkle there,
This fabric giggles without a care.

With every stitch, a joke unfolds,
As laughter in the fabric molds.
The colors play tag, bounce with glee,
In this woven comedy spree!

As shadows cast dramatic roles,
Each twist a punchline that consoles.
The weaver chuckles, takes a bow,
While the fabric laughs, 'Oh, wow!'

So take a leap in woven cheer,
Embrace the whimsy lurking near.
In this vibrant world, we find our way,
With radiant threads at play each day!

Chasing Glimmers Through the Veil

Behind the curtain, a shimmer peeks,
A giggling spirit, it softly sneaks.
It tickles the air, a playful tease,
As laughter dances in the breeze.

With glimmers bouncing like playful sprites,
It throws a party of dazzling lights.
Each twinkle winks, a cheeky grin,
Inviting all to join in the spin.

The veil shimmies with a sly delight,
Making mischief from day to night.
It hums a tune of quirky play,
As joy unfolds in a bright array.

So chase those glimmers, don't delay,
In this merry game where giggles sway.
For every smile, a sparkle's near,
In this realm of fun, all is clear!

Shimmering Patterns in the Mist

A twist and a turn, oh what a sight,
Patterns are dancing in the soft bite.
Threads are giggling, swaying so free,
In the mist, they play-tag with glee.

Frogs in bow ties are joining the show,
Spinning and hopping, they steal the glow.
What a grand mess of mischief they weave,
As whispers of laughter start to believe.

Polka dots prance like they own the place,
While swirls do a jig with a playful grace.
Oh, who thought coils could roll with such flair?
In this misty dance, jokes fill the air!

Chasing the shadows, we twirl and we toss,
In patterns of fun, there's never a loss.
With each little twinkle, the world seems so bright,
In this merry chaos, all feels just right.

A Dance of Shadows and Sparkles

In the corner of dusk, where giggles reside,
Shadows are bouncing, they take us for a ride.
Petals are clapping like children at play,
Sharing their secrets at the end of the day.

Glistening bugs spin in a comic ballet,
While clowns in a patch dance the night away.
Winks and bright nudges fill skies with delight,
As shadows pirouette, it's pure silly sight.

Fabrics of whimsy flutter and tease,
Frolicsome whispers ride on the breeze.
Each sparkle a wink, each shadow a jest,
Together they dance, bringing out their best.

So twirl in the twilight, let's tumble and roll,
With sparkles and shadows, we lose all control.
The night's full of surprises, a riot of fun,
In this dance of delight, we all come undone.

Luminous Pathways through Textiles

Woven with laughter, the fabrics excite,
Paths made of giggles illuminate the night.
Stitch by stitch, the nonsense unfolds,
With riddles and chuckles, their tales are told.

Banners of fun wave in soft, cozy air,
As patches of humor flit here and there.
We stroll past each fiber, each twinkle a friend,
Where since it began, it just won't end.

Tickles of sunshine burst through every seam,
While playful designs launch a whimsical dream.
Folks donning rainbow socks giggle and glide,
On these lively paths, let's all take a ride!

With curious threads leading us off the map,
In this land of wonder, we'll take a nap.
Not a dull moment, just joys every way,
In this handcrafted world, we laugh and we play.

Gardens of Subtle Illuminations

Underneath bushes, where mischief can brew,
Glow-in-the-dark critters peek out for a view.
They chuckle and scheme in the garden at night,
With giggles like fireworks, oh what a sight!

Every blossom a joke, every leaf a pun,
In this patch of giggles, we all come undone.
Frogs tap-dance alongside the wavy grass,
Each hop a tiny giggle—oh, how they pass!

With daffodils chatting and daisies that cheer,
We find hidden laughter tucked closely near.
In this garden of whimsy, we take our own flight,
As we twirl with the shadows, our hearts feel just right.

So let out a chortle beneath the moon's gleam,
In this world of laughter, we float like a dream.
With secrets of bloom dancing all around,
In these jovial patches, pure fun can be found!

Whispers of Fabric Under Stars

In shadows where the fabric hums,
It giggles softly, making fun of sums.
A misplaced stitch with a sense of flair,
Dances wildly in the cool night air.

The moon peers down, quite amused and sly,
As threads attempt to reach the sky.
With every twirl, a snicker is shared,
In a tale where no one is prepared.

A patchwork quilt dons a Snuggie crown,
It shuffles about, then flops on down.
The night is young, with all its quirks,
As fabrics prance and initiate smirks.

So let them weave in silly delight,
Beneath the stars, what a comical sight!
With every fold and every twist,
It's a tapestry where laughter can't be missed.

Glistening Patterns of Tomorrow

In the morning glow, they swirl and shine,
A parade of patterns, bold and fine.
One sock is stripy, the other square,
They giggle together, without a care.

A pattern's debate, bright checks or dots?
They tickle the seams of their little thoughts.
With every twist, a squeak of glee,
The fun unfolds like a quirky spree.

Tomorrow's threads in a playful dance,
Each fiber winks, gives fashion a chance.
They plot to outshine, oh what a feat,
In a world where mismatched is the ultimate treat!

So here's to the day, let's weave a tale,
Of patterns so wacky, they'll never fail.
Each stitch a giggle, a smile, a cheer,
In the realm of tomorrow, there's nothing to fear.

Sunkissed Entrancements

Beneath the sun, they sway and gleam,
Fabrics frolic, living the dream.
A curtain flutters, playing peek-a-boo,
While tablecloths tease, 'What's up with you?'

A sun hat chuckles, 'Look at my flair!'
While scarves twirl round with debonair care.
In the garden, they whisper with cheer,
Each petal blushing, 'Let's all gather here!'

With a wink and a flutter, they bounce about,
'Shall we play dress-up?' they gleefully shout.
Chasing butterflies, they sing and play,
In a world where drapery dreams the day away.

So join the fabric flair fiesta soon,
In the warmth of the sun, their fun's monsoon.
Layer upon layer, the laughter will rise,
In this fabric world under sunny skies.

The Sheen of Hidden Stories

With every fold, tales begin to weave,
A story of threads, you wouldn't believe.
The sparkles whisper of what's been said,
As patterns unfold from the edges of red.

In a closet, they gather, sharing a grin,
Each seam a secret, a playful spin.
The fabric of life holds wonderful dreams,
In the sheen of what laughter really means.

A mismatched quilt, a riot of fun,
Telling stories of all that they've done.
The button brigade, each one a sage,
Chortling loudly from their fine paper cage.

Let's dive into tales of the seams that bind,
In the hidden stories, cherish what we find.
So here's to the fabric that laughs in delight,
Each stitch a giggle, glowing through the night.

Glistening Whispers in Fabric

On a breezy day, a curtain sways,
Whispers of fabric in playful arrays.
A sock in the air, does a pirouette,
While the neighboring shirt thinks it's all set.

Ink spills on denim, oh what a sight,
The polka dot purse squeals with delight.
A scarf kisses boots, but they duck in a fright,
Who knew that these threads were ready to fight?

The sun peeks in with a warm teasing grin,
As aprons take bets on who'll fall in.
A tangle of dresses dance round the chair,
And one gets too frisky, jumps up in the air.

The mishaps of fabric, a comedic show,
In a world where seams and silliness flow.
When laundry day comes, it's pure, joyous cheer,
For the threads that connect us, year after year.

Flickering Hues of the Evening

As the sun waves goodbye, colors change hue,
A rogue blue sock just don't know what to do.
It sneaks through the darkness, all sly and aloof,
While a bright orange hoodie shouts, 'Hey, that's unproof!'

The twilight unfolds, draping shadows so bold,
The curtains conspire, their stories unfold.
With laughter they echo, and jokes they ignite,
As the stars fashion hats for the evening's delight.

A quilt starts to giggle, a blanket gives chase,
As the spoons in the drawer all dance with such grace.
In a bowl near the window, the fruits share a pun,
That the mischief in fabric is never quite done.

So, let's wrangle these colors and patterns with glee,
As the night winks and whispers, 'Just wait and see!'
In a tapestry woven with chuckles and cheer,
The evening's shenanigans sparkle so clear.

Tangled Threads of Dawn

At the crack of dawn, the ropes start to stir,
Knots in the shoelaces all start to confer.
The pillow sneezes, soft fluff in the air,
While the quilt plots a heist with a mischievous flair.

A sweater debates if it's too warm or not,
While the curtains play hide and seek from the pot.
The sun peeks in with its golden parade,
As dance-offs commence 'tween the socks that they laid.

An apron lounges, dreaming of pies,
While napkins snicker and roll their eyes.
The coffee pot chuckles, sending steam with a grin,
In a world of mischief, where laughter begins.

As dawn brings its colors, so bright and absurd,
The threads twist and twirl, their anthem unheard.
With each tangled moment, they frolic and play,
In a merry ensemble to start off the day.

Illuminated Whispers

Beneath the dim glow, a hat makes a speech,
While old scarves debate how many they can reach.
A button rolls laughter, as it bounces with glee,
While a pair of close friends, socks, share their key.

The sheets on the bed whisper secrets of night,
As they weave tales of dreams under stars shining bright.
The curtains all shimmer, in shades of great fun,
As the night spins its yarn under the playful sun.

A blanket trips lightly, trying to strut,
As mismatched gloves join the chaotic glut.
With every soft fluttering, laughter is shared,
In a world full of jest, it's love, unprepared.

With twinkling whispers, the fabric takes flight,
In shadows where fabrics dance, a sheer delight.
With joy intertwined, and chaos in sight,
The illuminated whispers unfold through the night.

www.ingramcontent.com/pod-product-compliance
Lightning Source LLC
Chambersburg PA
CBHW070311120526
44590CB00017B/2633